Albert Barnes

The Conditions of Peace

A Thanksgiving Discourse

Albert Barnes

The Conditions of Peace
A Thanksgiving Discourse

ISBN/EAN: 9783337115883

Printed in Europe, USA, Canada, Australia, Japan

Cover: Foto ©ninafisch / pixelio.de

More available books at **www.hansebooks.com**

THE CONDITIONS OF PEACE.

THANKSGIVING DISCOURSE.

BY

ALBERT BARNES.

much concerned that you
will say something that will
expose Harry

Pour out your thunder in
single notes —

They what have all Drunk

Katy did

Seymour & McClennan out of Bed

THE CONDITIONS OF PEACE.

A THANKSGIVING DISCOURSE

DELIVERED IN THE

FIRST PRESBYTERIAN CHURCH, PHILADELPHIA;

NOVEMBER 27, 1862.

BY

ALBERT BARNES.

PHILADELPHIA:

WILLIAM B. EVANS,

No. 1334 CHESTNUT STREET.

1863.

HENRY B. ASHMEAD, PRINTER,
Nos. 1102 and 1104 Sansom St.

CORRESPONDENCE.

SATURDAY.

Rev. ALBERT BARNES,
    REV. AND DEAR SIR: —

A very general desire is entertained by those who had the pleasure of listening to your Discourse upon Thanksgiving Day, that it should be printed. And many who from various causes were unable to be present when the Discourse was delivered, are anxious to consider and gain light and strength from the matured thoughts of one, for whom they not only feel a love and respect, but in whose judgment they repose great confidence.

We earnestly request, that you will, as early as convenient, furnish us with a copy of the Discourse, for publication, knowing that in so doing we but express the wish of many, and believing that good cannot fail to result therefrom.

With great respect,

November 29, 1862.   Your obedient servants,

AMBROSE WHITE,
WM. G. CROWELL,
SAMUEL H. PERKINS,
JAMES BAYARD,
JOHN SPARHAWK,
ALEXANDER FULLERTON,
JOSEPH B. LAPSLEY,
HENRY PERKINS,
ISAAC C. JONES, JR.,
J. S. KNEEDLER,
EDW. H. WILLIAMSON,
ROBT. EWING,
RICHARD C. DALE,
H. H. MEARS,
JNO. B. GEST,
CHARLES BROWN,
WILLIAM PURVES,
JAMES S. EARLE,
Q. CAMPBELL,
JOHN C. CLARK,
SAML. C. PERKINS,
ERSKINE HAZARD,
ABR. R. PERKINS,
F. L. BODINE.

GENTLEMEN : —

Your request for the Discourse delivered on the day of Thanksgiving, is a sufficient reason, whatever might be my own judgment in the case, for publishing it. As, however, from the great length of the Discourse, a considerable portion was omitted in the delivery, and, as it happened, that part of the Discourse concerning which there would be likely to be most difference of opinion about the correctness of the views presented, it would be unjust to hold any persons responsible for the sentiments advanced, but myself, and in yielding to your request, I desire that it may be understood that I alone am responsible for those sentiments. With this understanding—grateful that the address, as far as heard, so met your approval as to lead you to desire its publication, I yield it to you. Some of the views advanced may surprise my friends. Possibly on more mature reflection, I might see reason to change them :—possibly those to whom they might appear doubtful on their first suggestion, might on more reflection be led to regard them as true.

With great respect,

I am sincerely and truly yours,

ALBERT BARNES.

Messrs. AMBROSE WHITE,
  WM. G. CROWELL,
  SAMUEL II. PERKINS,
  JAMES BAYARD, and others.

DISCOURSE.

THERE never has been a time, in our own country, or in other countries, when, if a man had anything to say that could comfort, animate, or encourage his fellow-citizens, or had any claim derived from his age, his position, or his experience to impart counsel, it could be more appropriately done than now. Involved in a war such as has existed in no other nation; with numerous enemies to the government in every part of the land; with reverses that tend to humble us in our own eyes and before the world; with comparatively little progress in the great objects of the war; with a demand on the resources of the loyal part of the nation that test to the utmost its ability and its patriotism; when measures are adopted, most extreme in their nature, and that try to the extreme of endurance the loyalty of the people—measures submitted to as a temporary necessity, only because it is believed that there are greater interests that would be imperilled if they were not adopted; with no manifested sympathy among the nations of the earth, and with little real sympathy from any of those nations; with the nations of the old world looking greedily for the entire breaking up of our institutions, and the overthrow of a free government, the result of so much sacrifice and toil, and the last hope of free institutions on the earth; a contest in reference to which the people from whom we have sprung, whose language we speak, whose religion we have inherited, and whose blood flows in our veins, seem

most of all to rejoice at the prospect of our utter dis-
comfiture, rupture, and downfall; exulting in our disasters,
taunting us for a want of military and civil power and
skill, and, under a pretence of neutrality, really in alliance
with those who have risen in arms to overthrow the
government, and strangely sympathizing with an organization based avowedly on the perpetual subjugation of
one part of the race to the will of another,—under circumstances such as these we meet to-day to enquire what
there is to be thankful for; what there is to encourage
hope; what there is to cheer in the prospect of the
future; what should be done—what can *we* do for the
afflicted land that we love.

Without, I trust, any improper reference of a personal
nature, I may be permitted to say that I have reached a
period of life when a man *ought* to be able to make some
suggestions of value in such a crisis as this; when he ought
to be able to say something that might be well founded in
regard to the causes of such a state of things; to the
evils which have brought so great calamities upon the
land; to the remedies for those evils; to what may reason-
ably be hoped for in the future. I have, at any rate,
reached a period of life when I have little to hope or to
fear from my fellow-men; yet a period when a man, with
any right feeling, is conscious of a stronger love for his
country in proportion to the nearness of the time when he
is soon to be withdrawn from it. In such circumstances,
a man may venture on suggestions which would have been
less proper at an earlier period of life—suggestions, perhaps, not put forward with as much boldness and confidence as the suggestions of earlier years, yet, if he has
reflected at all aright, with a more comprehensive view of
the great issues at stake, and with deeper solemnity. He

who has little to hope for personally in this world; whose aspirations must be now so almost entirely in the world which he is soon to enter, may still cherish a hope for his country, for the church, and for mankind, not the less intense because the great blessings of religion and liberty are hereafter to be enjoyed by others, not by himself.

I shall venture, therefore, on this occasion to make some suggestions which I trust may not be improper, and which I am sure will be well received so far as the intention goes, in reference to what our country has been as one of the family of nations; to the grounds of grateful feelings to-day; and to what seems to me to be demanded for the restoration of peace. The suggestions will be loyal, but they will be free. In all my life I have defended freedom of speech, and fought many a battle for it. I have felt no restraint on that subject hitherto; I feel none now. I believe that when freedom of speech shall be taken away, the last hope of the nation—the last remnant of liberty, will be gone.

I believe that we have the best constitution, and the best mode of government in the world, and that it is the most wicked of all acts that man can do at home, and the most wicked of all things that nations can countenance abroad, to attempt to destroy that constitution, and to overthrow that government. And yet I believe that mistakes were made in framing that constitution, inevitable, it may have been, in the circumstances, which time has developed, and which have culminated in this most wicked rebellion; that there are evils contained in the constitution which it is possible still to remedy and remove, and which must be remedied and removed, if the great purposes of the formation of the constitution shall be carried out in a restored and permanent Union. Our fathers were not ignorant of the existence of those evils. They could not, or they supposed they could not, remove them. They hoped that time and wisdom, that the experience and the patriotism of the nation, would remove them. Time, progress, ambition, selfishness, conflicting interests, have developed the evil; rebellion has shown to us its magnitude ; the desolations of war, the tens of thousands slain on battle-fields, the tens of thousands maimed for life, the tens of thousands of families bereaved, the tens of thousands of graves newly made, where sleep those who have been called forth in defence of their country, show how great was the evil, and call on the nation to arise and re-adjust our institutions in accordance with the eternal principles of righteousness. It may be that those evils *could* be removed only by the baptism of fire and of blood through which our nation is now passing.

The past in our history is fixed, and so fixed that, in the main, coming times will not reproach us; in such a way that foreign nations, however much they may now desire it, could not find occasion to exult over us. " The past," said Mr. Webster, in relation to a part of our country—to Massachusetts—" The past, at least, is secure. There is Boston, and Concord, and Lexington, and Bunker Hill, and there they will remain forever. The bones of her sons, falling in the great struggle for Independence, now lie mingled with the soil of every State, from New England to Georgia; and there they will lie forever."* So we may say, in similar respects, of our whole country ; of our whole history. There is

---

* *Speeches*, vol. i, p. 407.

Plymouth, there are Yorktown, and Saratoga, and Trenton, and Princeton, and there they will remain forever.

Thus, too, it is with the history of our fathers; with the settlement of our country; with the perils, the sacrifices, the self-denials, of those who came to this western world to found a new empire; to establish institutions that should be free. Foreign nations cannot now go back and reproach us for what our fathers were, nor for what they did. Reproach for those who drove them out, and who compelled them to leave their own land, then a land of oppression, there is enough of in history, and the judgment of the world on that subject is not to be reversed. The world knows by heart the history of the men that came to this continent. It understands the reasons why they came. It has learned the character of their principles, and the extent of their sufferings. It knows what they did, and that record is engraved as in eternal brass. England, with all that is bitter in her feelings now, cannot be suffered, and will not be suffered, to go back and change the judgment of mankind in regard to the reasons why the Pilgrims left her shores, or what they did in penetrating the forests of the New World. No nation has ever had such a commencement of its history as ours :— so pure, so noble, so self-sacrificing, so comprehensive and far-reaching in the principles of the men who founded it. Not Egypt, nor Assyria, nor Babylon, nor Greece, nor Rome; not among the ancients, nor among the moderns, has there been a beginning in respect to which there will be so much which the world in its better days will be glad to retain in its history; one which it will be so unwilling to "let die."

The past is fixed too as we would desire it should be, in regard to the establishment of the Independence of our country. It was not hasty; not rash; not ill-advised. It was not the result of passion; nor did it spring from any ill-feeling toward the mother-country, or any desire of doing her wrong. It was a measure resorted to after a long series of oppressions and wrongs, and after appeal and remonstrance had proved to be vain. To the British Sovereign; to the British Parliament; to the British nation, those appeals and remonstrances had been made long, and continued to be made till the last hope of their being effectual, even in the minds of those most reluctant to engage in war, had died away.

And the war of Independence itself was such that the nation has no cause to look upon it with shame; nor has history anything to record in regard to it to our reproach. It was not, on our part, a war of barbarism; it was not conducted by calling in the aid of the scalping-knife and the tomahawk; it was not stained by bad faith, or by dishonorable deeds; it was not conducted on principles that subject us to just reproach among the nations. No great revolution was ever conducted with so little to give pain or cause regret in the recollection; no war has been waged at any time in which there was so little to give just offence, or to shock the moral sense of mankind.

The past is fixed, and fixed, in the main, as we should desire it to be, in regard to the organization of the government of the country *as* Independent. It was done in a peaceful manner; it was done when the highest wisdom of the nation was summoned to calm and deliberate investigation. Not a measure was adopted as the result of force or of fear; not a provision was put into the constitution at the instigation of the bayonet. Never before in the history of the world was there assembled such a body of men for the purpose of framing a constitution for the government of a great country, and never before has there been seen in our world a spectacle so sublime as pertaining to the origin of a nation, as when that constitution was submitted to the calm judgment of a people then numbering three millions. In securing its adoption, not a vote was forced; no man voted because he was afraid to vote otherwise; no man voted because his vote had been bought.

To the formation of that constitution, and to the constitution itself, we now look with gratitude, with pride, as the chief, the crown of the blessings which God has given to this land. To say that it has *no* defects, is what no American has ever been required to say; to say that it *could* not be made better, would be to deny the very principles of the constitution itself, for it has made provision for its own amendment. Our fathers were sagacious enough to see that there were evils existing which there was not then power to remove, but which it was hoped time and good feeling might remove; they saw that among a people destined to grow and to spread over a vast extent of territory there might be provisions desirable which had not occurred to them; they saw that in the unknown future, when a comparatively small population should be multiplied to hundreds of millions; when a vast expanse of forest should be subdued, and become the abode of civilized men; when rivers and lakes then unexplored even so as to give their course or outline on a map, should bear on their bosoms the productions of a teeming soil; when the commerce of the infant nation might whiten every sea, and new relations might spring up with other nations of the earth, there *might* be occasion for change, and it *might* be proper to

appeal to the wisdom of the nation and examine the
new state of things which would demand the change.
The constitution, we may admit, was not perfect. But
it was the noblest and the best that the world had seen.
It has made us great. It has developed our resources.
It has made us respected and feared wherever it was
desirable that we should be respected and feared. It
has created for us a navy; it has created a commerce;
it has saved us from border wars; it has made the
North what it is, and the South what it is; the great
West what it is, and what neither could have been but
for the constitution.

The past is fixed in regard to our treatment of the
nations of the old world, and fixed in a manner which
we have little to regret, and little that we might wish
now to have changed. We have desired sincerely to be
with all those nations, at peace. We have been disposed
to make equal and just treaties with them in regard to commerce. We have sought to take no improper advantage
of them. We have been willing to visit with them every
distant sea, and every distant port, and to share with
them in the fair avails of commerce. We have impressed
none of their seamen into our service. We have made
no war on their peaceful pursuits. We have never
intermeddled with their affairs, but have aimed to stand
not merely professedly but really aloof from all the
conflicts which they have waged among themselves; to
maintain not a hollow and hypocritical, but a real neutrality in regard to the wars, right or wrong, in which
they have been engaged. We have seen them often
waging what we regarded as unjust wars. We have
seen them invading peaceful nations. We have seen
them attempt to suppress insurrection and rebellion in

their own provinces by means that, as a christian and civilized people, we could not but regard as barbarous and cruel—in a manner, that, in the language of the Earl of Chatham, when describing a measure which had been deliberately proposed in the House of Lords to be pursued in reference to the revolted colonies of America, "shocked us as lovers of honorable war, and as detesters of murderous barbarity." We have seen them binding men to the cannon's mouth, and sweeping them by scores into eternity. We have seen them, for the purpose of compelling a foreign nation to admit as an article of commerce and of consumption, against their own just and humane laws, a drug most deleterious to the bodies and the souls of men—destructive to morals; destructive to religion; destructive to domestic peace; destructive to national progress—waging a fearful, a bloody, and a horrid war, until the object was accomplished, and the ports of the greatest nation in the world were compelled to be thrown open to admit that, in commerce, which would spread wo, and sorrow, and wretchedness everywhere. We have not interfered. We have not even taken part with the oppressed and the wronged. We have not, in a public and national manner, uttered the language of remonstrance at such barbarities and atrocities. We did indeed interpose when Scio was laid waste by fire and sword, and her beautiful villas and gardens were smoking ruins; when the oliveyards of the Peloponnesus were cut down, and the Turk had laid all waste; when Greece, once the land of beauty and the home of civilization and art, was suffering all the ills of famine from the desolation of ruthless war—*then* we interfered by the noble resolution in Congress, and the noble speech of Mr. Webster, and by contributions, not of arms and implements of death, but of food for the famishing, from churches, and villages, and private citizens, to relieve those sufferers. And when the scourge of famine and pestilence swept over Ireland, and England failed to supply the wants of the famishing, we did interfere—we hastened to relieve them : an act which Ireland has never forgotten, but which England has. Beyond things like these we have not ventured to interfere in the affairs of nations, remote or near ; and in regard to nations, we have at least the consciousness that in our treatment of them we have endeavored to carry out the great principles which we have designed to lay at the foundation of our own prosperity, that justice, and truth, and honesty are the best foundation of a nation's progress, as they are of the welfare of an individual—that "righteousness exalteth a nation." That we are innocent in regard to all men—to those within our own borders—the Indian, the African, we cannot indeed affirm ; to foreign nations our course has not been one of dishonor and shame, and we are willing that it should be known and read by all men.

In all these respects we look with special pleasure and approbation on our treatment of the land of our fathers. England has been dear to us. There are the graves of the ancestors of our Carvers, our Brewsters, our Hancocks, and our Adamses—of our Henrys, and our Pinckneys —of Washington. Its language is ours. Its religion is ours. Its history is ours. We delight to think that Milton, and Cowper, and Shakespeare, and Newton, and Bacon, are no more theirs than ours. We visit that land with emotions such as we can have toward no other land —save Palestine, and in Westminster Abbey we sit down and weep, for there we are surrounded by the monuments, and tread on the graves of the illustrious dead whose names and works have been familiar to us from our cradles. We have not been unwilling to bear much from England; and to forget all the past, when we could show to her respect and affection. We welcomed the Heir apparent to her throne to our shores, and gave him an "ovation" in the land, not forced and formal, but hearty and sincere, for the nation honored and respected the pure and virtuous character of her that bare him, and wished well to him and to the land where he would occupy the throne.

The past is fixed, and fixed in the main as we would desire it should be, in regard to the manner in which the resources of this land have been developed; to our growth and our greatness. That we have been proud of this; that we have boasted of it; that we have attributed it to ourselves; that we have felt that we might defy the world; that we have supposed that nothing could now retard our progress; and that, with all that there has been of greatness in that which was good, there has sprung up a rank and pestilential growth of evil corresponding in some measure with the magnitude of the good, we are not disposed to deny.

But still, the nation *has* become great; greater than any other nation has ever become in the same period of time; great, in the main, in the right direction. No other nation has ever advanced so rapidly, or developed such resources in the same period of time. Not Egypt; not Assyria; not Babylon; not Persia under Cyrus and his successors; not Greece; not Rome; not Germany, Gaul, or Britain. Britain:—it was long and slow from the time of the Druids, from the time of Alfred, from the time of William the Red-haired, before the resources of the little island were in any measure developed—more than a thousand years from the time of Alfred. We might have hoped that England would have looked on, with gratification, at the amazing development here of institutions and of power, derived in a great measure from herself, and among those who spoke her own language. For the development here was in the same *line* as that which had made England, small in territory, great in wealth, in influence, and in power. It was a development in agricultural improvements, in schools, in colleges, in the comforts of life, in intelligence, in liberty, in religion, in commerce, in labor-saving inventions. We had carried out in our *purposes* all that we had derived of *good* from the mother country; we had endeavored to avoid that which was *evil* in her example, and to prevent the ill consequences of what she had entailed upon us. All that had been good in her learning, her religion, her laws, her literature, her morals, her arts, we were endeavoring to make our own, and to spread them as rapidly as possible over the vast domain which God had put in our possession, and we have done it to an extent which the world has never before seen. The evil which there had been in the memory of former things, and the evil in her example, and the evil which she had entailed upon us, we were endeavoring to avoid and remove. We had forgotten, as a people, the history of her persecutions—those persecutions which oppressed our ancestors, and which drove them out on the wide and stormy ocean in frail barks, to an uninhabited wilderness, and we were willing that those things should pass from our memory, and from the memory of mankind; saying, in kindness to the people of the mother country, as Joseph did to his brethren, "As for you, ye thought

evil against us, but God meant it unto good." Gen. 1. 20.
We had seen evil in some of the institutions of the mother
country, in her form of government, in her aristocracy,
in her oppression of the poor, and we endeavored to
avoid them, and to carry out, in free institutions, her
own ideas of liberty. We did not inherit, perhaps partly
from the necessity of the case, since God gave us, without a war of conquest, more territory than we know what
to do with, her love of conquest, and we meant to live in
peace with all the world. There was, indeed, and there
is, one great evil which we had inherited, which has been
our bane and the cause of all our trouble, which we had
not, up to the war, been able to remove. Our fathers complained that England had forced it upon us. It was an
original charge in the Declaration of Independence, that
this had been forced upon the Colonies without their
consent. England was more responsible for it than we
were. Those unhappy foreigners of a different skin had
been conveyed here in British ships, and under British
laws, and in the use of British capital, and for the purposes of British gain. The suppression of the trade was
then demanded by no developed principle in the British
constitution, and by no prevailing feeling of the British
people. It was long, long after this, that the case of Somer-
set occurred, in which it was determined that slavery
in England was contrary to the British constitution, and
the delivery of the opinion of Lord Mansfield in that case
constituted an epoch in English history. But the evil
was already entailed upon us, and the great principle
which was thus, at a late period, announced in England,
came *too late* to reach the evil which she had inaugurated
in the Colonies, for then we were an independent people.
Oh! how happy had it been for us, for England, for

2

Africa, for the world, if Mansfield had lived a century earlier; if a similar case had occurred then; and if the great sentiment of liberty which went forth when he uttered that memorable opinion, had covered the *colonies* as well as the little parent isle—that sentence which proclaimed that, " The air of England has long been too pure for a slave, and every man is free who breathes it. Every man who comes into England is entitled to the protection of English laws, whatever oppression he may heretofore have suffered, and whatever may be the color of his skin :—

Quamvis ille niger, quamvis tu candidus esses."*

But the evil was fastened upon us. It had struck its roots deep. It threatened to fill the land. We have not been able to remove it, and when we failed from want of power, or want of will, or both, God took the matter into his own hands:—and on the throes, and conflicts, and stripes, and blood, and sacrifice, and sorrow, incident to it, England looks without sympathy, without any manifested regard for her own principles, apparently willing now that the curse which she entailed upon us shall rend our Republic, break down forever our free institutions, and bathe the land which she has herself twice endeavored in vain to conquer, in oceans of blood.

We may not boast. We have not been, and are not, as a nation, what we should be; but we may say *without* boasting, and in grateful language appropriate to this day, that the sun has yet to shine upon a land where there has been more public and private virtue; where there has been more domestic peace and tranquillity; where there has been a wider influence of education;

* Lord Campbell's Lives of the Chief Justices of England, vol. ii. p. 231.

where the obligation of contracts has been more sacredly
regarded; where there is more respect to law as law;
where there is greater security of property or of personal
rights; where there is, on the whole, as much purity of
religion; where there is so much happiness springing
from the virtues of domestic life. There has been, there
is, no land where an unprotected female could travel so
far, and meet with so much attention, and be so safe from
rudeness. There is no land where so large a proportion
of the population can read and keep accounts. There is
no land where the laws can be so easily executed without the representatives and the insignia of military power.
There is no land where life and property are so safe. I
passed, as thousands of others have done, and still do,
the early years of my life in a quiet home, on whose
doors and windows there never had been a lock, or bolt,
or a fastening of any kind—not even a nail; and where a
peaceful and industrious family lived for more than half
a century, without fear, alarm, or peril. To what other
land will men go—save it may be Switzerland, where
scenes like these are common?

So much for the years that have gone by, and whose
results have ceased to be our particular history, and have
passed into the general history of the world.

We meet to-day, especially, to recall the mercies of
another year. It too is now passed, with all that it had
for us of joy or sorrow, prosperity or adversity, peace or
war, laughing or tears, sleep, rest, toil, trouble, anxiety,
bereavement, gain, loss, public grief, or private sorrow.
It has been such a year as our country has never ex-
perienced before, and will make more work for the calm
and impartial historian of future times, than any one year

in all our public history. For there are sad things to be recorded which *may* not look as sad as they now do, when they are fairly recorded; things to be explained, which cannot now be explained; reverses to be set in a true light, whose causes cannot now be understood; plans broken, defeated, or accomplished, not now understood, which are to have an important bearing on our future history, and whose bearings can only be seen *in* that future. There are men, who, during this year have made their first appearance on the stage of human affairs, whose life, plans, and purposes may exert a most important influence on the future history of the world; men whose characters are not yet understood, and whose acts can be explained only in future times when the smoke and mist which now envelop them shall pass away, and there shall be the return of a clear and unclouded sky:—for the land has not only been enveloped in the smoke and dust of battle, but the campaigns, the plans, the victories—why any, why not more; the characters and purposes of many of the actors in these scenes, are as yet enveloped in smoke and dust *like* the battle-field. There have been reverses such as no nation with similar power and resources ever knew; and there have been great deeds which will make the year memorable among all the years of our history. No man commends his own wisdom who pretends now to understand the events of this passing year.

There have been scenes, indeed, which have filled the land with sorrow, for the central part of our land is almost one great hospital or graveyard, and desolation has marched over great tracts which were before the scene of quiet homes, and green fields, and orchards; the peaceful places of churches and schools. If this were a day for fasting, humiliation, and prayer, it would *seem* to be much easier to find topics appropriate for *such* a day than for a day of thankfulness to God ; nor should we *forget* this while we endeavor to *find* topics for devout acknowledgment of the divine goodness. "It is a good thing to give thanks unto the Lord," and man can always find, if he will, that for which his heart should rise in gratitude to his Maker.

Personally, life, health, food, raiment, home, friends, social blessings ; the Providence which has kept us in the ways of virtue, honesty, and truth ; the advances which we may have made in knowledge ; the tranquil hours that we have spent ; the support we have had in trouble ; the blessings of salvation and the hope of heaven ; the fact that all along through the year God has been merciful to our unrighteousness, and has been willing to hear our prayers in all circumstances, and to save our souls,—all these and kindred things should rise up to remembrance as we recall the events of another year.

Our land, too, even amidst the desolating scenes of war, has yielded abundance. Half a million and more of men have been withdrawn from the peaceful pursuits of life, and have been in tents, or without tents, away from their homes ; and these too, in the main, composed of that class who do the hard work of the field, the ploughing, sowing, reaping, and gathering into barns ; yet in our Northern States it does not appear that an acre less than usual has been cultivated, and never have the fields yielded a more abundant harvest ; never have the orchards been borne down with more abundant fruits ; never in our history has there been, strange as it may seem, a greater amount of exports of those things needful for life.

The year has been a year remarkable for health, for freedom from the ravages, even the local ravages of disease. Not as in other years have we been summoned to sympathize with portions of our country visited with pestilential diseases, and to send or go, that those in attendance on the sick and the dying, might themselves become martyrs in the cause of kindness and charity.

Our land, in schools, colleges, churches, seminaries of learning, is still a prosperous and a happy land. Those schools have not been broken up; those colleges have not been disbanded—not even one closed by war; those churches, though diminished in many cases in the numbers sent and drawn for the field, are not closed; those seminaries of learning, for the youths of either sex, for agriculture, for preparation in the studies of the professions—law, medicine, divinity, are scarcely even checked in the career of providing for the wants of the next generation.

The nation, in all these things, in all that *makes* a nation prosperous, is prosperous even amidst these scenes of war, and there is not now on the face of the globe a land in passing through which a stranger would see everywhere so many evidences of domestic peace, of happy homes, of successful agriculture, of life, and energy, and activity, in the marts of business, or on the wharves of commerce, as in this land, even amidst all that is sad and desolating in war.

We have been enabled to maintain peace with the world at large; to secure the sympathy and kindness of some of them; to check the outrages and wrongs of others; to hold them at a distance when they threatened us; to calm their rage by successful acts of diplomacy and by just explanations when they were ready to make war upon us; to prevent a recognition of the portion of our land engaged in this great rebellion, even when the attempt has been made to show that every interest of foreigners, and all the concentrated hatred of our prosperity and of our institutions, and all the long-cherished desire of our division and our ruin, demanded such a recognition. In future times it will be regarded as *among* the most memorable things in this year that the Independence of the Southern Confederacy was *not* recognized abroad, and that the affairs of our nation have been so wisely conducted in this respect, that God could properly so interpose and stay the wrath and the desires of interest, and hatred, and of jealousy, as to prevent a recognition which *might* have severed our Union forever, and which *would* have involved us in conflicts with the powers of the old world, and perhaps have kindled a universal war.

The power of the government to sustain itself, and the disposition of the nation *to* sustain it, have been evinced. If during the year, now closing, we have not done all that we hoped to do; if there have been mistakes and errors in conducting the war; if there have been sad and mortifying reverses, it is still true that the rebellion has *not* been successful, and still apparent to ourselves and to the world that this government—this constitution —is settled on a foundation which no mere power of man can overthrow. Never in the history of the world has there been so formidable a rebellion as this, and never has there been a year which so much tried the strength of a government as this year has tried the strength of ours. Extraordinary measures have indeed been adopted—measures regarded by a part of the people, even of the friends of the administration, as perilous to liberty, and not sanctioned by the constitution; and endured only because they were regarded as *necessary* for the time, and, therefore, in the willingness to submit to such measures even for a time, furnishing one of the strongest proofs of the true amount of patriotism in the hearts of the people; but none of these things has had power to change the settled purpose of the nation to maintain the Union and the Constitution, and to restore peace by any expenditure of treasure and of blood that may be necessary. On this point there is at present but one voice at the North; and the formation of parties is not based on the question whether the war shall or shall not be prosecuted, and whether the government shall or shall not be sustained. I consider this firm purpose to sustain the government; to defend the country; to place at the disposal of the government all the money, and all the men that may be necessary to sustain its operations by land and by sea, as one of the most remarkable events in the history of the world, and one of the best evidences of the freedom, and at the same time of the vigor of the government. The year which is now closing *may* yet be regarded as among the most remarkable in the history of the world, as thus testing the power of a Republic, and answering the question so often asked with no friendly spirit abroad, whether Republican Institutions can be permanent; whether nations have the power of self-government. If this government can go through this war without being overthrown, there is no earthly power that it will have reason to fear, at home or abroad. Foreign nations see this; and with anxiety, and hatred, and hope, they are watching this struggle as decisive of what they have to fear in the working of their own institutions, and what they may have to fear if they provoke a war hereafter with the American people.

Perhaps most of all as adapted to shape the future history of our country, and to make this year remembered with gratitude by those who love the liberty of man, it may be regarded as most eventful in breaking the bonds of servitude, and removing the great evil— the cause of all our troubles. In the din and conflict of battle; in the anxiety which all have felt in regard to the armies summoned from the people—the anxiety of fathers, and mothers, and wives, and brothers, and sisters, about those dear to them exposed to the perils of the camp; in the wail of sorrow which has come up from all parts of the land; in the records of victories and defeats, keeping the attention of the nation fixed most intensely on one object, there may have been scenes enacted which have scarcely attracted attention, which will go more deeply into the future welfare of the nation than any events which have occurred in former times, and which, now occurring almost without notice, could not have been secured before without the danger of a revolution. Twenty years ago it required all the talent, the eloquence, and the influence of John Quincy Adams, to dare to present to Congress a petition for the abolition of slavery in the District of Columbia, and a law to that effect then would have involved the nation in a civil war. This year it has been done; and so quietly and calmly that the nation has been scarcely aware of it: and yet it is done; it cannot be undone. The Territories—the vast Territories—of the nation, hereafter to be great States larger than many of the kingdoms of the old world, are *free*, and, as territories, they are to be free forever from the tread of the slave;

from laws reducing men to chattels; from laws which authorize the traffic in the bodies and souls of men: yet who almost is aware of it? Who has heard a voice of thanksgiving for it? Who has reverently paused in the din of arms, and the surges of war, to thank God for it?

A blow has been given to the slave trade this year such as has never been struck before. It was indeed piracy by our laws, and by the laws of other nations; but it was piracy on paper only. In our principal marts of commerce, and under the influence of men most prominent for station, and wealth, and enterprise, vessels were freely fitted out for this traffic, and the infamous men engaged in the traffic were allowed to go at large with impunity. It needed an example to show that *anything* was meant by our paper laws, and that we were not dealing falsely with mankind in proclaiming the traffic to be piracy; and it needed, and it found, one man who had firmness enough to carry out the principle, and to show what the nation understood by the term as applied to that species of commerce, and at last one guilty man for this crime has suffered the just penalty of the law. A great movement, such as this nation has never before seen, has been suggested and recommended on the subject of emancipation. Never before has a suggestion on that subject been made by a President of the United States; never before commended to Congress; never before received the sanction of the Representatives of the people: and yet it was so wise, so calm, so free from any attempt at compulsion; it so left it to the States themselves; it offered such a fair compensation; it would have such ultimate influences if acted on, as, in the very form in which it was submitted, to constitute an epoch in the history of our country. It was an epoch in the history of England when a member of Parliament ventured to suggest the idea of Emancipation in the British colonies: it was much more when a President of the United States ventured to use the term, and to suggest the idea, as a practical one. And then this year will be still more remarkable for things not yet recorded; whose bearings are not yet seen; whose influence on this subject is to go far into future times: things which, whatever may be the issue of the present conflict, will make new adjustments necessary. Slavery is not what it was; it will never be what it was again. The Fugitive Slave Law is not what it was; it can never be what it was again. The slave all along the Border States is a different being from what he was; is more of a man; is less a "chattel" and a "thing;" is of less value as "property" than he was, or ever will be again. The power springing from this source, which once, and so long, controlled the nation, is broken, and, whatever may be the issue of this struggle, is not to be a controlling power again. Thousands, and tens of thousands, have tasted of freedom who never knew it before, and we begin to look on to times when the land shall be free. Could we now see what the future patriot will see; could we see all the secret influences at work this year for the good of the nation; could we see all those deep and broad streams of liberty and happiness which will flow out to future times to fertilize and bless the land and the world: no language which we can use now would be such as would properly express the praise due to God for what may spring out of the events of this year. Our minds are indeed pensive and filled with sadness. Our eyes "pour out tears unto God." But there is light beyond; and those who will live in the future, may see, even in what gives us sorrow now, reasons for adoration and praise in a land made more happy; a land without our conflicts and troubles; a land where man shall be everywhere recognized and treated *as* a man; a land that shall be truly free.

The past is fixed; and we should be grateful to-day. The future is to us now the great source of solicitude and anxiety. This dreadful war! When will it end? How will it end? What good will be accomplished by it? What compensation can there be for all this blood and treasure—for all these woes and sorrows? What will be the condition of our country *when* it is ended? Shall we be one, or two, or many; a people with one government; one constitution; one purpose: or a broken people with no government, and no constitution; a people destined to perpetual border wars, or a people, all our liberties gone, to be collected into one, if ever one again, under a military despotism? We cannot but ask these questions with anxious hearts; we cannot answer them; we cannot find anything that will calm the mind but in the belief that there is a God, and that the God of our Fathers, having now, as he had in their troubled days, his own plans, can and will interpose as he did then. At his feet we are safe; and at his feet we may be calm, and there, with humbled hearts, having learned great and valuable lessons in regard to our pride, and self-sufficiency, and dependence, it is his manifest purpose to bring us. When we are actually brought there, with right feelings, then, and not till then, may we "look up," for then we may feel that "the day of our redemption draweth nigh."

But can we see nothing now to inspire hope? Can we

see nothing that may be changed for the better by the war? Can we see no evils in the past that this fearful struggle is likely to correct? Can we not see what *would* conduce to permanent peace, and what would prevent a recurrence in future times of such fearful and bloody conflicts? Valuable above what our fathers left us, rich as was that inheritance, will be the legacy which we of this generation shall leave to after times, if we can leave a government, a constitution, where the causes of collision will be removed, and those evils which have been culminating for eighty years will exist no more.

There will be peace. This war, among a people of the same language, the same religion, the same interests, will not last always; will not last long. All men must see that it must come to an end; all see that it must come to an end at no distant period.

There will be great results that will come out of the war. It is indeed true that war not always, perhaps rarely, affects the great points immediately at issue; but it is also true that there are other results invaluable to mankind that spring indirectly out of war. There are few great principles of liberty in our institutions, or in the world, whose establishment has not been effected as the result of bloody wars: principles that are worth to mankind all which they have cost; whose influence in promoting the happiness of the world is more than a compensation for all the treasure and blood expended— as the blessings of Christianity are more than an equivalent to mankind for all the toils of apostles, and the sufferings of martyrs.

But can any one suggest now what would be the conditions of a permanent peace; what would remove forever the causes of war and alienation; what would be equal justice to all, to the North and the South; to humanity; to the world? May we venture to suggest, to what point things are tending; can any one venture to paint and describe some of the "shadows" which coming events are forming, and of which the outlines may begin to be apparent?

It cannot be the recognition of the Southern Confederacy. In such a recognition, under any form, and with any conceivable arrangement, there must remain the occasions for war, for constantly recurring appeals to arms. Apart from the principle, the asserted *right* of Secession which this would involve, and which might be as proper in any other case as the present; apart from the public recognition as right of all the treason in high places, the robbery, and the wrongs done to the nation's property and the nation's honor, there would be things which could never be adjusted to the idea of peace and concord. With fifteen hundred or two thousand miles of coterminous territory, requiring vigilance at every mile in collecting the revenues, and everywhere furnishing occasions of collision; with different views of trade and commerce; with great rivers flowing across any possible boundaries, and whose navigation would be necessary for the prosperity of either portion; with the different institutions of freedom and slavery coming constantly into collision; with no common regulations in regard to commerce and trade; with no united strength as presented to the nations abroad; with no national credit; with no national navy; with no national name, there could not be arrangements for permanent peace.

It is equally clear that there cannot be permanent peace under the arrangements which have existed heretofore; even those which have been admitted into the constitution. The same causes would again produce the same effects. This war is not accidental. It is not a sudden outbreak. It is not the result of individual ambition. There are things in the frame of the government which have tended, under existing circumstances, to produce it, and which would produce it again. There are evils whose growth could not be checked by any provisions in the constitution; evils which mere time could not remedy. No man is bound by any proper principles of loyalty to say that the constitution is perfect; no man exposes himself to any just charge of disloyalty to say that it might be amended to advantage; no man is now in the interest of the rebellion who ventures to say that the amended Constitution of the "Southern Confederacy" has provisions which it would be well to introduce into the General Constitution of the Union.

It is not strange that in an instrument like that of the Constitution of the United States, a re-adjustment might be demanded. Our fathers, as already remarked, wise as they were, saw this, admitted it, made provision for it. But few years passed away, as yet without any painful collision, but anticipating such a possible collision, when it was found necessary to apply the principle, and at no period has it been regarded as showing any disrespect to that immortal instrument, to suggest that it might be amended. After eighty years in which its practical workings have been seen; after the wonders which have been wrought under it; after all the proofs of amazing wisdom in its general structure and provisions; after all that it has done to give us a place among the nations of the earth; and after the experience of the evils which have resulted from a few of its provisions, as now developed in scenes of dreadful carnage and blood, assuredly there should be wisdom and patriotism enough in the North and the South to attempt a re-adjustment; to secure the just rights of all; to remove, forever, if possible, the causes of collision and war.

What would such arrangements be? May a man, not a politician; not a statesman; devoted from early years to other pursuits; having no claims to be heard beyond that small circle whom his official position entitles him to address, or whose ear he may have gained by a life spent in the honest desire to do good to mankind; yet a man who, in humble imitation of the great statesman, would desire that "when his eyes shall be turned to behold, for the last time, the sun in heaven, he may not see him shining on the broken and dishonored fragments of a once glorious Union; on States dissevered, discordant, belligerent; on a land rent with civil feuds, or drenched in fraternal blood,"—may such a man, in his place, *suggest* what would seem to him to be demanded as the conditions and terms of abiding peace?

The first great principle in the return of peace, must be the suppression of this rebellion as rebellion. It must be founded on the laying down of hostile arms by those who have made war on the flag of the nation; the restoration of forts and arsenals, and public property, seized by force or fraud; the recognition of the laws of the Union; the abandonment of the whole principle in regard to the right of Secession. In all cases of rebellion, there must be a submission to just authority before there can be proposals and conditions of peace. God treats with men in rebellion only when they submit to authority and law; and a government that recognizes a conspiracy and a rebellion, and which treats with it *as* such, is already at an end. The throne of God would have long since crumbled to atoms, and the universe would have long since been chaotic and anarchical, if any other principle had been recognized in the divine administration than that of submission to the just and equal laws of heaven. The welfare of the nation; its name, its power, its credit, its influence, and the happiness of innumerable millions on this continent, all demand that this great principle shall be settled now and forever, that there is a " GOVERN-MENT" here; that it *is* a government in the highest sense of the term; that under that government, and in its proper operation, it has *power* to enforce its own laws, and to extend its control, under constitutional limits, all over the land. The immediate question now is, whether that can be done; the solution of that question is to determine the destiny of this nation for all coming time. The duty now, the immediate duty, the sole duty, is to suppress this rebellion, and to establish the authority of law; to maintain the Union. That, and that only, is the purpose of the war. That, and that only, makes the war right. That, and that only, will make its issues safe. Any thing else; even any scheme of benevolence; any measure based on the intrinsic wrong of slavery; any thing that contemplates the amelioration of the condition of any portion of the population; any act of justice to the oppressed and the wronged as such; any redressing of old grievances, or any rendering of tardy justice long delayed; any proposed amendments of the constitution as a *basis* or a promised *pledge*, valuable as they might be in themselves, and incidental as they may be in the prosecution of the war, would be aside from its design; would be a violation of the constitution; would properly subject an Executive to impeachment. There is one object before the nation now, and but one: those rebel-

lious men must be beaten on the battle-field; those forts
and arsenals must be restored; those custom-houses must
be put again under the control of the nation; those
armies must be dispersed; those new laws, which are not
laws, of the "Confederacy," must be abrogated; the
honored old flag must float again over every part of the
land, before there can be permanent peace. "No other
measure than this will preserve the integrity, the dignity,
and the glory of this government. No other measure
will prove to the world that we are what we profess to
be—A NATION. No other will settle this controversy on
a lasting basis." Failing here, we fail altogether, and
the cherished hopes of our fathers will have vanished
forever; and the exultation of those, who beyond the
seas hate liberty, and us as the representatives of
liberty, will be complete.

The second thing is the preservation of the Union.
Men talk traitorously when they speak with complacency of
the breaking up of this Union. The old thirteen States,
under the articles of the Confederation, and before the
Federal Union was formed, found themselves unable to
carry on the operations of a government. They had no
government, no army, no navy, no credit, no power.
The Southern Confederacy would have no power now,
were it not for the pressure of the war which keeps them
together. It is the Union which has made us, and which
has kept us. We must be one great nation, or twenty
or more divided, and separate, and jarring, feeble powers.
We must be one in respect to war, and peace, and commerce, and trade, and credit; we must be one in view of
ourselves, one in view of the world. Besides, who would
be authorized to propose peace on any other terms or
conditions than the preservation of the Union? Who has

been chosen by the people for any such purpose? Who, under the constitution, has any such authority? Within the proper limits of whose oath of office would it come that he should propose or listen to a separation of this Union? What officer in the nation could do this without a usurpation of power never conceded to him, and fatal to liberty?

The third thing essential to permanent peace must be the entire suppression of the slave-trade. Whatever may be true in regard to the moral character of the traffic, it is clear, that in this age of the world, and in the condition of the public opinion in the great mass of the people of this nation, peace and harmony could not exist if this traffic were re-opened and continued in any part of the nation. The intrinsic wrong of the traffic, as it appears to one part of the nation, bringing the power of conscience against it, and the supposed interest of the other part of the nation, urging its continuance, must produce a renewal of the conflict, and to secure permanent peace, it must be in fact abandoned forever. This has been, is, and must be, the settled purpose of the nation before the world. This was the settled purpose of those who framed the constitution when they incorporated a provision that this should *not* be done before a certain period—the year 1808—implying that it might be done, and should be done then; this is the avowed principle, whether sincere or otherwise, of the so-called " Confederacy;" this is now the settled purpose of the Government of the United States, declared not only in laws, but in the execution of a guilty man engaged in that horrid traffic. And this must be. The age demands it. Humanity demands it. The Bible demands it. The best interests of the nation demand it.

Our standing among the nations of the earth requires it. The common character of the nation; the common welfare of the community; justice, mercy, religion, all demand that human flesh, among all nations, shall be separated from all those things which pertain to lawful commerce, and the traffic in it branded as the worst form of piracy. As the world would be shocked, and the nations would feel that they had a right to interfere, should either France, or England, or Portugal, or Spain, engage in piracy, or countenance or protect it by law; so, with equal right, might the nations of the earth interfere should any one of those engage in the slave-trade. The prohibition of this traffic could not, therefore, be complained of in any part of our country as a sectional, and partial, and unequal arrangement, for it lies back of any sectional and local bearing, as that which pertains to justice, to morality, to humanity; to every ground of a claim to a name and place among the nations of the earth. There *are* eternal principles of right, and they are becoming incorporated, slowly it may be, but certainly, into the code of the laws which are to regulate nations; and as it would not be partial, sectional, or unjust, if a portion of Northern citizens should desire to engage in acts of piracy, and should regard it as for their interest to be permitted to fit out piratical vessels from their ports, if they were prohibited by national laws on the ground of justice, humanity, the law of God, and the common good, so it is not, and would not be a sectional act, or a partial act, to prohibit the slave-trade to each and every part of the nation. For any new adjustment of the constitution this should be adopted as a settled principle, proclaiming now before the world, not only that Congress *may* pass laws prohibiting the traffic in human flesh, but that the trade shall be forever abolished, and that no laws favoring it shall ever be enacted in the United States.

A fourth thing, now shown, by the terrible war into which we are plunged, to be essential to permanent peace, and demanded alike by the best interests of the North and the South, and by every principle of just government, is the entire separation of the General Government from slavery. This, I regard, as THE great principle necessary in the restoration of peace; the great principle on which the constitution, if ever amended, is to be amended, and on which, if ever, the liberties of our country are to be preserved. Except in the matter just referred to, of prohibiting the slave-trade, the principle should be made universal that the General Government should have no relation to slavery; should in no wise protect it; should in no manner interfere with it to abolish it; should derive no benefit from it; should lend it no support; should in all respects, and at all times, stand wholly aloof from it. The South demands this in words, at least; the North should yield it; the nation— the world—humanity—justice—national honor—religion —should insist on it forever.

The great evil in this nation, the source of all our national woes, consisted in incorporating with the constitution *any* provisions whatever, save in the matter pertaining to the slave-trade, in relation to slavery. This principle, in my judgment, is so important—so vital to permanent peace; so demanded by every sentiment of national honor and justice, that I may be permitted to dwell on it for a moment.

There are three provisions now in the constitution expressed or assumed, on this subject, which lie at the foundation of all our difficulties; which are unjust to the

North and to the South; which are in violation of all the principles of humanity—of what is due to man as man; which are the source of endless contentions and strifes; which originated this dreadful war; which go far to explain the anomalous and strange position of foreign nations towards us:—provisions which stir up all that there is of interest on the one side, of conscience on the other, and of hatred on both, and which bring us as a nation into constant collision with the law, the government, and the Providence of God.

Those provisions are: 1. That slaves, considered mainly as property, shall constitute a basis of representation in Congress, in the proportion of three-fifths of their number; 2. That the power of the General Government shall be employed in restoring fugitives from slavery; and, 3. That Congress has the power, and the right, to prohibit slavery in the Territories of the nation. . This latter is an implied or assumed claim. A remark or two on each of these, will explain more particularly what I mean.

1. For the first of these: That the African race, held in slavery, shall be represented in Congress in the proportion of three-fifths of their number. This is not, indeed, a direct *representation* of the African race themselves, for in the constitution they are not so far regarded as *persons* as to have the rights of citizens, and of course any *right* to be represented in Congress. The representation is based on the idea of *property;* to wit, that they *are* property, and that *as* property, there may be an additional representation in Congress from the Slave States.* This was one of the "*compromises*" of

---

* "It is only under the pretext that the laws have transformed the negroes into subjects of property, that a place is assigned them in the computation of numbers; and it is admitted, *that if the laws were to restore the rights which*

the constitution, and the essential idea was, that, in order to secure something like a just *balance* between the North and the South, *persons* only should be the basis of representation in the North; persons *and* property, to wit, property in slaves, should be the basis of representation in the South.* This, according to the ratio of representation now in congress, would give to the South, on the basis of *property* about twenty additional members in Congress. If the *property* idea, so unjust, were laid out of view; if those of African descent at the South were treated as they are at the North, and as on every just principle they should be; if the same principle were adopted in the Slave States as in the Free States, that, in the words of the constitution, "Representatives shall be apportioned among the several States which may be included in this Union, according *to their respective numbers ;*" if all who are held in slavery were treated in this respect as persons and not as property, then the South would be entitled to an additional representation in Congress, in proportion to the two-fifths of all who are now held

have been taken away, the negroes could no longer be refused an equal share of representation with the other inhabitants." *Mr. Madison*, in the *Federalist*, No. LIV.

* "In settling the ratio of representation, another difficulty arose respecting the slaves, who form so large a portion of the inhabitants of some of the States. To compute them among the number represented, would be giving them an importance to which their character did not entitle them ; * * * * to omit them altogether, in the computation, would be to reduce the influence of the Southern States, in a manner to which they would never consent. As a medium between these, it was agreed that five slaves should be accounted as three citizens, in arranging the representation, and the apportionment computed accordingly. To counterbalance, in some degree, this concession to the Southern States, direct taxes are to be apportioned by the same rule as representation ; so that the same cause which increases their influence in the national Legislature, subjects them to the necessity of making larger contributions to the national treasury, when that mode of taxation is resorted to." *Bayard on the Constitution of the United States*, pp. 49, 50.

in bondage, and in no way represented in Congress. On every principle of justice and equity this should be done, and this is undoubtedly a case, and so far as I can see, the only case in which a palpable *wrong* has been done to the South in the constitution. Of this, however, they have not complained, and could not complain, without renouncing what they regard as *essential* in their Institution, the right of *property* in men.

2. The second of the provisions in the constitution in regard to the relation of the General Government to slavery, to which I have referred, is that by which fugitives from slavery are to be restored to their masters. The article in itself, as originally adopted, and as it stands in the constitution, is merely that " No person held to service or labor in one State under the laws thereof, escaping into another, shall, in consequence of any law or regulation therein, be discharged from such service or labor; but shall be delivered up on claim of the party to whom such service or labor is due :"—that is, that their return or restoration shall not be prevented or hindered by any laws in the respective States on the subject; or, in other words, that the masters shall have the power and the right to reclaim them, without any interference on the part of another State to prevent it ; of course always implying that the claim shall be fairly made out. This simple provision, bad enough in itself, has been perverted and abused by being made the foundation of the most odious and iniquitous law perhaps ever enacted in any christian country, by which the whole power of the General Government is pledged to the return of such fugitives; by which it is made the duty of every man to render aid in such a return ; by which fine and imprisonment may be the penalty in any

case of refusing to render such aid, or for assisting a fellow-man to escape from bondage, and to become a freeman:—that is, for refusing, in a christian country, to violate what he may conscientiously believe to be an explicit law of God on the subject, "Thou shalt not deliver unto his master the servant which is escaped from his master unto thee."* This law has been, indeed, pronounced on high authority—the highest in the land—to be *constitutional;* that is, not in fact a *violation* of the constitution, but still, it has never been shown that a *milder* law embracing *all* that was fairly implied in the constitutional provision, would *not* also be constitutional; in other words, that a law might not have been so framed that, while it maintained all that is required by the letter of the constitution, it would not have required free citizens to do what would be a violation of their consciences, a law which would have been less palpably a violation of the law of God. More than any other one enactment—more than any other one cause—this law, in the form in which it exists, has been the cause of the alienation of the North from the South.

3. The other form of jurisdiction of the General Government on the subject of slavery, is the power claimed for Congress, and exercised by Congress, of excluding slavery by law from the Territories of the nation. This power, not expressly granted in the con-stitution, and not necessarily implied in the general pro-vision that "The Congress shall have power to dispose of, and make all needful rules and regulations respecting the Territory or other property belonging to the United States," (Art. IV. Section iii. 2,) has been claimed at the

---

* Deut. xxiii. 15.   So, also, Isa. xvi. 4: "Let mine outcasts dwell with thee; be thou a covert to them from the face of the spoiler."

North; has been denied at the South; was exercised by Congress, with scarcely a dissenting voice, in the case of the Territory North-West of the Ohio ceded by Virginia; was implied in the Missouri compromise; and was among the *immediate* causes of the trouble which led to this unhappy war. And yet, notwithstanding all these acts and decisions of so high authority, it *may* yet appear that it is a power which Congress never had; which it was never contemplated that it should have under the constitution; and which is fundamentally erroneous in regard to all just principles of legislation. The power to prohibit slavery may imply the power to ordain or establish it; and if Congress has this power in one respect, it would be difficult to show why it has it not in the other. Slavery is, in all cases, the mere creation of the laws: the laws of war; the laws of rapine; the laws of crime; the laws of complexion or race—or laws founded on those things. It does not exist by nature. It is not founded on any natural rights. It does not go anywhere by any natural right, or by any natural law. It is always the creation of law—of local or municipal law; and in all places where it is not *ordained*, or made such by *law*, MAN IS AND SHOULD BE FREE. Such are now understood to be settled and admitted principles; and as in the "Territories" Congress alone has power to make laws, or to "legislate," and as Congress has no power to make men slaves, or to institute slavery, so it follows that all the inhabitants of the Territories are free as long as they remain Territories; free, that is, until the people acting for themselves shall ordain otherwise. The right to *prohibit* slavery must go with the power to enact or ordain it; and Congress has neither. It is for the people alone to determine this; but whether *when* so determined any new State shall be admitted into the Union is another question. *If* so admitted, the matter is, and should be with them alone.

These are the provisions in the constitution, expressed or implied; provisions claimed, denied, perverted, abused, which have been the source of all our national woes.

But what is the effect of these provisions in the constitution? What is there that should make it desirable that they should be changed?

The first of these questions now claims attention. The other will be answered in the other specifications which I have yet to suggest.

The effects are obvious:—the evils are palpable, at home; abroad.

AT HOME. Recognizing, as the constitution is supposed to do, the right of the General Government to interfere in the matter at all; the fact that slavery as property is represented in the General Government; the right and the duty of the General Government to employ its power, civil, military, and naval, if necessary, in restoring fugitive slaves; the right of the General Government to legislate on the subject of slavery in the Territories, the effects are obvious. The constitution *seems* to be the defender of slavery. The South is clamorous for the interposition of that power in its behalf. It is jealous, and properly so, of any measures that would divide, abridge, or diminish the exercise of the power of the General Government in defending, extending, and perpetuating the Institution. It claims, and fairly too, that the power of the nation, as expressly prescribed, shall be exerted to the full extent conceded in the constitution; it demands that all that is vague and undefined shall be determined in a manner not against the interests of the Slave Power.

The North, too, feels, and justly, that under this arrangement of the constitution, it has interests and responsibilities of a most grave and momentous character in the matter. It is not so much the interest of the tariff, of commerce, and of manufactures—of cotton, tobacco, and sugar—it is the interest springing from conscience and from national responsibility. Just so far as the subject pertains to the National Government, and just so far as the North constitutes a part of the nation, so far, under the constitution, the North *has* an interest in it; so far it has a right to discuss it; so far it has a right to prevent any aggressions which the slave power might make; so far it has a right, in common with the other portions of the country, to deal with it, under the limits of the constitution, as it has to deal with the army and the navy—with the public lands, the Postal arrangements, and the Customs. It is *not* a meddlesome interference with "domestic" institutions; with what does not pertain to us, when, as far as it is recognized and sustained by the National Government, it becomes a subject for examination and discussion. We interfere with no man's rights; we invade no man's prerogatives; we do nothing in violation of any rights of States, when, as long, and as far as it is a National Institution, or is sustained by the National Government, we examine freely the whole subject of slavery. And so long as the arrangement exists; so long as it is incorporated into the National Constitution, there will be two great parties—the one uniting with the South, and from pretended or real love of the constitution, or of the love of power, urging the demands of slavery; the other based on opposition to the idea that the National Government is to be governed by slavery, to submit to its control and demands, to extend it, or to do anything to perpetuate it—a party always necessarily advancing toward the idea that the National Government has the power to abolish it, and should do it. To a large part of a free people also, and especially a people in any degree under the dominion of *conscience,* it is a source of constant irritation that by a fair interpretation of their own acts in legislation, and by arrangements which are claimed to exist in the very constitution, they are compelled to approve of measures which go to sustain an institution which they regard as a direct violation of all the principles of humanity, and of the law of God.

ABROAD. It is not to be wondered at that our institutions have never been well understood abroad. To say nothing of a very prevailing ignorance in the older nations of Europe on all subjects, these institutions are, in some respects, so complicated; they seem, in the relations of the General Government and the several States, to come so much into collision; they are so unlike all which exists in the Old World, that we are not to wonder at the fact that they are not understood. Especially is this true in regard to slavery. That many of the people of foreign lands have great pleasure in maligning and misrepresenting us, and in hailing any indication of the downfall of the Republic, is undoubtedly true; and that much that is said on our position now, and much of the sympathy shown for the South, by those who have claimed to be pre-eminently the friends of liberty and the enemies of slavery, proceeds from this cause, no one will venture to deny.

But there *are* honest minds abroad, and there may be minds there not inimical to our country, and which are in fact drawn toward us by the strong ties of consanguinity and religion, which are filled with deep perplexity on the subject, and with the deeper perplexity *because* they are opposed to slavery, and *because* they sincerely desire to see the great principles of the British constitution as expounded by Lord Mansfield, and as acted out in the emancipation secured by Clarkson and Wilberforce, extended over the world. On the one hand, they see, or think they see, that the constitution of this country is pledged to the support of slavery; they see that slavery is recognized in the representation in Congress; they see such protection in the Fugitive Slave Law; they think they see it in the Dred Scott Decision; they see it, or think they see it, even in the President's Proclamation; they see it, or think they see it, in the purposes of one of the great political parties of the nation now rising again into power; and they think they see that the triumph of the national arms—the suppression of the Rebellion—the restoration of the Union *as it was*, will carry with it all those arrangements by which the power of the nation was pledged to the defence of the institution. On the other hand, they think they see in the success of the Confederate Government, as circumstances must and will exist, the prospect of the speedy destruction of the system. Well as they know—for they cannot but know—the avowed principle on which that Confederacy is founded—slavery—avowed slavery—yet they see, or think they see, that, hemmed in as it would be; surrounded on every side by free States; with no power to reclaim fugitive slaves; with a border of some two thousand miles with nothing but imaginary lines, or creeks and rivers easily crossed, there could be no security for slavery; that the value of a slave *on* that border would soon diminish to nothing; that there is no such attachment to slavery among slaves themselves as to keep them from availing themselves of the facilities of freedom; and that slavery *must*, therefore, soon come to an end. On the one hand, they see, or think they see, nothing but that which aims at its perpetuity; on the other, while they see that it is the *avowed* purpose to sustain it, they imagine that they see that which in the nature of things *must* at no distant period lead to its abolition.* I confess that it seems to me that an intelligent foreigner—a true friend of human freedom—*might* be much perplexed on this subject; and that, with all that is justly to be said and lamented in regard to the bad spirit manifested abroad, it is *possible* for a true lover of our country, in its best interests, to look enquiringly, if not favorably, on the efforts of the Southern Confederacy, *because* he might suppose that he saw in that the only hope of the speedy removal of that great curse from our land, and from the world.

However this may be, and however the expression of this thought as coming from this pulpit may be received and regarded, yet there is—there can be no doubt of the fact that the complicity of the National Government with slavery may be, and is, one great cause among good men abroad of the want of sympathy in the efforts of the National Government to put down this dreadful rebellion. We shall stand upright before the world; we shall meet the demands of human nature in this age; we shall secure

---

* "We would ask what has maintained, unmitigated, the horrors of slavery in spite of the public opinion of the world? The protection of the North." *Edinburgh Review*, October, 1862, pp. 281, 282.

"We are convinced that the chances of mitigating and abolishing slavery in the Southern States will, if those States succeed in establishing themselves as a separate federation, be greater than such chances are if their conquest is effected by the arms of the North."—*Ibid.* p. 284.

"We cannot desire to see the Union re-established as a mighty power for maintaining slavery as one of its institutions within, and protecting it against all the nations of the world without."—*Ibid.* p. 285.

the entire sympathy of the lovers of freedom every where; I may say that we shall secure the perfect sympathy towards us of Russia, France, Germany, England, Scotland, Ireland, Italy too—yea, *Austria* it may be, only when with the clear note of freedom, with a manly and distinct tone, with an unambiguous utterance of the national conviction, and not as a mere military necessity, we shall repeat again before the world our solemn declaration, that "all men are created equal; that they are endowed by their Creator with certain unalienable rights; that among these are life, *liberty*, and the pursuit of happiness"—when we shall proclaim that the National Government is separated from slavery; that slavery is not represented in it as property; that the civil tribunals of the nation, its marshals, its military and naval forces, are not to be employed in arresting fugitives from bondage; that citizens, free themselves, are not to be subjected to imprisonment or fines for declining to aid in returning human beings, guiltless of crime, to chains; when we shall announce to mankind, with no uncertain sound, our belief as a nation that "God has made of one blood all nations of men to dwell on all the face of the earth;" that all have been redeemed by the same sacrifice on the cross; that every human being who has no other crime than that of "having a skin not colored like that of other men" is entitled to liberty.

A fifth principle demanded by justice, and necessary for the permanent peace of the nation, is, that representation in the National Government shall be uniformly at the North and the South on the basis of population and not of property. It is now wholly so at the North; it is partly so at the South. At the North, all, of all colors and conditions, except "Indians not taxed," constitute the basis in the apportionment of members in Congress. At the South,

as we have seen, all white persons, and three-fifths of all
held as slaves, are the basis. Those three-fifths, more-
over, are represented not as *persons,* but as *property.*
Two-fifths of the four millions of the inhabitants of the
South who are held in servitude, enter in no form into
the idea of representation, and contribute in no way to
constitute a Congress of the nation.

Ours is a Representative Government. But what is
that? It is based on human beings—on persons; not
on things—on chattels—on cattle. The essential idea
in all just notions of representation is, that where in all
the limits of the territory under the government there is
a human being, or one who has by nature the rights of a
man, and who in any way contributes to constitute the
nation as such, in its existence or greatness, there shall
be a suitable recognition of that fact in the representation in the government; and that, in this respect, as he
has by nature the rights of a man, and as his life, liberty,
and property may be affected by the government, he
shall be regarded and treated *as* a human being, as part
and parcel of the great Confederation.

As matters are now, gross injustice is done to every
part of the nation ; gross injustice to ourselves in the
eyes of the world. The North proclaims the principle
in relation to their Southern brethren—a principle not
recognized among themselves—that *property* may be in
part the basis of representation, and they concede to
Southern slaveholders what they claim, that their slaves
shall be regarded as *property,* and this odious principle
the nation proclaims abroad to the whole world : the
North, thus, with all its zeal for freedom; with all its pro-
fessed abhorrence of slavery; with all its deep conviction
that the African is a *man* like other men, yet declaring its

4

willingness that the only representation which there shall
be of a human being when a slave—the only recognition
of him in the halls of legislation, shall be as "*property*"—
as property and nothing else. Meantime, by a compromise unjust in principle, and inadequate in its influence,
the North has been all the while deriving an undue
advantage from this arrangement. In order to counterbalance the "concession to the Southern States" that
their slaves might be represented in the proportion of
three-fifths of their number as property, it was among
the unhappy "compromises" of the constitution, that
"direct taxes should be apportioned by the same rule as
representation." And as the Confederation in 1783 had
made it a rule in taxation that the direct taxes should be
apportioned on the principle that three-fifths of the
slave population was to be reckoned, it was deemed just
that the same principle should be adopted in settling the
number of representatives.* But since direct taxes
under our government occur at very distant intervals,
and since the representation in Congress is constant, the
North has been all the while reaping this advantage
over the South, paying little in the way of the compensation, and yet constantly enjoying the advantage in
Congress derived from the imperfect and unequal representation in the South.

In the mean time, the South has been suffering this
wrong—that, as now constituted, two-fifths of the
population, that is of what are now four millions of its
population, have been without any representation: in
other words, under the ratio of representation, there
has been a loss to them of ten, fifteen, or twenty members
of Congress.

* *Curtis's History of the Constitution.* Vol. ii. pp. 48. 160.

The true principle of representation would be, undoubtedly, that no human beings should be represented as property; that the apportionment should be in accordance to the entire population as reported by the census-tables; that whatever may be the domestic *relations* of such persons, or whatever their condition, as sick or well, old or young, ignorant or learned, male or female, bond or free, white, copper-colored, black, or semi-black, their existence as human beings—as a part of the nation—as having rights and interests as human beings to be protected—should be recognized in the government under which they live. In the carrying out of this principle, it is, of course, not *necessary* that all should be eligible to office, nor that all should vote; not that children, or slaves, or Indians, should be admitted as law-makers of the land. At the North the people regulate this in their own way: so let them do at the South. As at the North we do not choose that all persons shall be voters; and as we make distinctions—some of them arbitrary and unjust—yet all within our power—so let them do at the South. If they do not choose that the slaves shall *vote*, let it be so—let them treat them as *we* treat the colored population of the North; but in the name of humanity and of God, let them not be treated as chattels and things by an odious principle; in the name of justice and of equity, let not the North derive an advantage from an arrangement founded on a principle which the people of the North no where else recognize—the right of property in man; in the name of justice too and equal rights, let the South be entitled to *all* the representation which she could claim based on the Census—on the actual numbers of human beings—men, women, and children within the limits of the respective States.

A sixth thing:—The ultimate entire removal of slavery from our land is essential to permanent peace. Our history, under the Confederation, and now for eighty years under the Constitution, has shown that slavery has been, and is, almost the only cause of alienation between the North and the South, and that but for this there never has been any insuperable reason why the North and the South should not live and act in harmony. Indeed, on the entire surface of the globe there is no one country of such an extent, or of any very considerable extent, where there are so many causes for *unity;* so few for *division.* Of one language; one religion; one origin; one general character;—united by vast rivers, and by the advantages which each derives from the peculiar productions of the other; united in their history, and by all the sacred recollections of the remembered war of Independence, there is every reason, in the nature of the case, why we should be one. Our fathers felt this; and hence our glorious Constitution was formed, and we should have been now with nothing necessarily producing alienation, collision, or war, had it not been for slavery. But the same causes which have now produced collision on this subject will produce it again; nor will it ever be possible to adjust our free institutions to the idea that slavery is to be perpetual in the land. That fact is now established; it cannot be denied. The South knows it; the North affirms it; the world sees it. All attempts, therefore, to secure permanent peace except on the assumption that slavery is somehow to cease ultimately in the land, have been demonstrated by our past history to be vain.

Yet it is clear that in securing this result, everything must depend on the mode in which it is done—if ever done. It cannot be secured by a mere exertion of power; by an act from any quarter declaring all the slaves at once free. Such a power is not given to any individual, or to any body of men under the constitution, and however that power may be believed, in a state of war, to be "a military necessity," yet even this could extend *only* to those parts of the country actually in a state of insurrection, and could have no applicability to the portions of the nation that could by any fair construction be regarded as loyal. As a civil act; as an act pertaining to the General Government, Congress has no such power; the Executive has no such power; the third branch of the government—the Supreme Court—has no such power. Most foreigners, and especially those in the land from which we have derived our origin, and in a great measure our notions of liberty and government,* ignorantly, strangely, wilfully fail to comprehend our constitution on this subject; and they persevere in a determination not to be instructed. England, regarding her constitution as the perfection and sum of all wisdom, can *never* be made to understand why or how there should be a Government without "a King, Lords, and Commons;" or how there can be a Union of *States* which is not exactly like the union of the counties of Durham, York, and Lancaster; or like England and Wales; or on some such principle as that which unites Scotland and Ireland to the crown; or how there can be possibly in another land a legislative body that is not formed after the exact "pattern" of the British Parliament. Hence thus far in eighty years we have never been able so to instruct them that they will see that an American Congress has not the same power over slavery in the States which the British Parliament has over a poor-

* They understand us much better in France.

house in the counties of Cornwall or Kent, or as the same Parliament had over slavery in the British West Indies. They will not yet understand that *no* authority whatever in regard to the direct emancipation of slaves has been given to the General Government of our nation; and it is, perhaps, now too late to hope that they ever will understand this. At home this *is* understood; and it is, therefore, understood that any attempt to emancipate the slaves in this country by a mere act of the General Government would be an usurpation of power never conceded, and equally at the North and the South would destroy all hope of an adjustment of our difficulties. Besides, if this power were possessed by the General Government, and should be exercised by it, no pen could describe the evils which would follow from the immediate emancipation of four millions of people held in slavery: a people unused to freedom; most of whom are unable to read; a people unaccustomed to provide for themselves; having none of that economy which springs from the effort at self-support and the support of families; restrained now and habitually mainly by terror and authority, and not by conscience; and with all the remembered wrongs committed against them and their fathers. Such an act of immediate emancipation would, in all human probability, deluge the land in blood, and wrap it in flames. On the other hand, no tongue could describe the blessings which might flow from a wise system of gradual emancipation: where the end was distinctly contemplated, at no remote period, and where a system of training preparatory to it should be at once entered on, fitting those millions for freedom. Such an act would stand forth to the world as among the noblest of human achievements—greater than the deliverance of the children of Israel from Egyptian bondage; greater than the achievement of the Independence of our country—for the numbers are larger than in either of these cases, and the wisdom and the power needful would not be less than in either.

But the act of emancipation, if it occurs, should be an act in which the nation, as such, should, in every part, while claiming no right of direct legislation, bear its share of the burden. Slavery has been, to a certain extent, national. The disgrace has been national. The wrong has been national—so far as the Constitution has protected it; and, so far as ships fitted out in Northern ports, and merchants in Northern cities, have been enriched by the traffic in human sinews, it has been national. Bristol and Newport in Rhode Island, Boston, New York, Philadelphia, have had their share in the profits of the slave-trade. Splendid abodes now stand in Bristol and Newport whose foundations were laid in blood, and whose walls were reared as the result of the slave-trade. Wall Street would never have been what it now is, and New York might not as yet have travelled far beyond Canal Street if it had not been that Whitney—a northern man—gave cotton to the world, and if the South had not been willing that, on certain well-understood terms, their money affairs should be in the hands of the merchants and brokers of New York. Whatever there has been in fact as the result of slave labor, has gone, among other things, directly or indirectly to promote our growth as a nation; and whatever there is of power in this country now to affect the manufactures, the trade, the commerce of the old world has had a connection of melancholy importance with slavery. At this moment, England, France, and Germany throughout all her borders; the manufactures and the trade not only in Lancashire, but through the countries where the Elbe, the Rhine, and the Danube flow, *all* feel the effect of the want of that which is the result of slave labor—cotton :—and all begin to learn a lesson which they have been slow to learn, and which it would be well for them to learn in other respects than this—how greatly they are dependent on the United States; how important is the position which the United States holds in the world; how vital it may be for them to cultivate friendly relations with us.

As in some measure, therefore, a national matter; as that which has contributed to the greatness of the nation, and which has gone materially to enrich it, it is but just that when so vital a change is contemplated as the ultimate emancipation of four millions of men, every part of the *nation* should bear its share of the burden; every part of the nation should help to undo the wrong. *Compensation*, therefore, in accordance with some equitable rule to those States and individuals which would be immediately affected by it, is demanded by every principle of justice; by everything in our nature which responds to the claim of what is reciprocal and right. It is not, indeed, as a matter of *property*; it need not recognize the right of property in human beings. The claim is founded rather on a principle of equity, as springing from the fact that when, from any revolution in a nation's opinions and policy, a material change is to be produced in that which men have regarded as contributing to their prosperity, and of which the nation has been in any way a participant, every part of the nation, enriched by that which is to be of value no more, should bear its part of the loss and the burden. This may not be a legal claim. It may not be a claim which we place under the head of strict justice or right. But it is a claim which appeals to noble minds, and noble hearts—that where there has been a common wrong, and when there is now to be a suffering party, that party should not be left to suffer alone. It is, therefore, on the strictest principles of *moral* equity that it has been proposed by the highest authority of this nation, that there shall be a fair system of compensation proposed for the States which are willing to inaugurate a system of gradual emancipation.

Nor will it be a "compromise" with slavery, nor an acknowledgment that slavery is in itself right, if the system proposed should be *gradual*. Provided that the end is contemplated; that the thing is to be done; that arrangements are made to *do* it, and to do it certainly; that there is no further defence of it, and no further arrangements to perpetuate and extend it; that the announcement goes forth to the world that it is the purpose of the nation that slavery shall cease, there can be no fair construction of such an act by which it can be inferred that the system is regarded as right. In such an act there would be no mercenary apology for slavery; nay, the purest benevolence may mingle in the act, though it is delayed, for the highest interest of the enslaved himself may demand that delay. New York, New Jersey, Pennsylvania, uttered no voice in favor of slavery, and made no compromise with it, when they inaugurated a system of gradual emancipation, and the deeply-rooted feeling of those States on the subject is proof that there was no lingering love of the system in the legislation which prompted to those acts.

Nor is it needful to any just views of emancipation that the freed-men under such a system, or under any system, should be expatriated, or removed by power to other lands. This is their native land, and they love it. The four millions of slaves in our country, excepting the few scores that may have been smuggled in contrary to the laws, were born here, and have as good a right here as any others, for the "boundaries of their habitation" have been fixed here by the great God. Beyond most other men, too, the African loves his native soil. He has no disposition to leave the place where he has been reared, and where he has toiled—even for others; or even to leave those for whom he has toiled, if he is not treated with harshness and cruelty. In all that vast territory where the African has been compelled to toil, he would be a useful and a needed laborer:—not less useful, and not less needed, if, as a freeman, trained to freedom, he should be compensated as other men are for his labor. Free labor in an African would be of more value to a country than slave labor, and on the vast cotton fields and rice plantations of the South it may always be true that the African can perform a work which the white man could not endure. There, as freemen, let them live and labor, enjoying the avails of their labor as other men do; represented in the National Government as a part of the population of the land; recognized and treated as made in the image of God. If they prefer, as freemen, to return to the land of their fathers' sepulchres, let us help them. To other lands now barbarous and savage, not driven there, not compelled to go, they might bear, as they would bear, juster notions of industry, and thrift, and liberty, and religion than now prevail there; and colonies voluntarily formed, and sustained by those who have oppressed them, might be the means of establishing there the institutions of civilization, religion, and the arts.

Africa, blessed by the voluntary return of her sons, may yet forget the wrongs that have been done to her, and slavery may yet be numbered among the evils that have been overruled by divine Providence for the good of mankind.

A sixth principle, founded on such views as have now been presented, and claimed, it seems to me, with exact justice by the South, is that slavery as to its CONTROL, and as to all the laws regulating it, is to be left to the States as such, in all respects, absolutely and exclusively.

It is a settled principle in all just laws, now admitted everywhere, as already remarked, that slavery is only a creation of law; that it is not a condition of nature; and that where there is no law to make a man a slave, he is free. If it be by the laws of war, if it be by the laws of debt, if it be by laws pertaining to crime; then those laws, and those alone, define the existence, the locality, and the extent of the bondage or servitude of man. Just or unjust, then, the regulation is a municipal regulation, and the institution is a "domestic" institution, and as such it should be left to the States themselves. Like other local matters—things of domestic concern, it should be limited there, and when those bounds over which those domestic laws extend are passed, then any human being should breathe the air which other men breathe. Men at the South have claimed that we have no right to interfere with their institutions. As far as they and we have made them a *national* concern, we have such a right, for so far it pertains to us as it does to them. But let it be so; let it be as they desire; let slavery be a local institution; let it be like other domestic arrangements; let it be wholly detached from all connection with the General Government; let all laws in relation to it outside of the respective States where it exists cease, and cease forever. Beyond that right which all men have to spread abroad light and truth; to diffuse their sentiments as they may; to publish books, to preach the gospel, to persuade men to do what is right, and to avoid what is wrong, let there be no asserted right of interference; let there be no interference. Let it be placed on the same footing in this respect, as other matters that relate to the interests of the people of the land. It is rare that any of our interests, of persons, property, liberty, reputation, come in direct contact with the General Government. The ordinary course of affairs in which all are interested, is through the State considered in this respect as sovereign. "It is to the State Government that a man looks to protect his property, and secure his personal safety. It is the State Government which makes the laws that affect all his daily transactions, and it is the tribunals of the State Government which decide all the ordinary questions arising between man and man." Thus let slavery be.—This is no unholy compromise of truth; it is no compromise at all, farther than when we seek to spread truth and learning, liberty and religion, in Turkey, or India, or Burmah, or China, or Italy, by the gospel, we go under an implied pledge not to attempt a direct interference with the laws—the local laws of these lands.

One other principle, as following from these views, remains to be stated. It is, that the entire subject of restoring fugitive slaves should be a matter of negotiation and arrangement between the States themselves. If as States independent in such matters, as in other local matters, they can enter into such negotiations and arrangements, well; if not, let not the power of the

General Government be prostituted and profaned in the work of arresting men who pant for freedom; let not its judges "pollute the purity of the ermine" by remanding freemen to bondage; let not the army of the nation be employed to force their return at the point of the bayonet. Let no conscientious and peaceful citizen be required to engage under severe pains and penalties in reducing men and women to slavery. Let not the Government of the United States continue to place itself in this false position before the world, the only free government on earth, and yet the only government in all the nations that binds itself to do such a deed.

As the South claim that this is an institution of their own with which we have no right to intermeddle, let it be so. Let us not volunteer to interfere. If they can make an arrangement with Border States, equally independent in such subjects, an arrangement for their reciprocal good, well; if not, let that be an end of the matter. If such States acquiesce in this; if they deem it just to others, or best for themselves, let them do it in their own way, and on their own responsibility, and let the Fugitive Slave Law be blotted from the statute book of the nation forever and ever.

I know that I have been too long in this service; but neither you nor I will ever attend a Thanksgiving service in such circumstances again. I have seldom, if ever in my life, spoken with so much diffidence or distrust, in regard to the sentiments which I have felt it my duty to advance. That these sentiments will be regarded as practically wise by any considerable portion of those whom I have addressed, or adopted by the country, I am not sanguine in believing. That they are more just in describing the evil, than wise in proposing a remedy, perhaps I should be as readily disposed to grant, as any would to assert. But these things which I will now suggest in a few words, would follow if the nation should ever admit the propriety of these principles; and the prospect, however dim it may now be that they will occur, should be a cause of thanksgiving, just in proportion as the eye of faith or patriotism can see *any* evidence that they will occur.

The nation would be one; there would be one flag, one system of laws, one religion; we should be one people.

The occasion for war, so far as it has sprung from slavery, and there has been no other occasion for war in this nation, would cease, and we might hope would cease forever.

The conscience of the North would be relieved, as having no further complicity with slavery, and as being henceforward in no way responsible for it:—conscience, the most troublesome thing in a nation to manage, the most difficult to be subdued.

The rights of the South would be secured—secured in what they regard *as* their rights; secured in that of which they are deprived—a just and equal representation in Congress; secured as to any invasion from the North on their institutions; secured in what they choose to regard as valuable domestic arrangements; secured in regard to any direct interference with arrangements which they think proper to cherish.

As a nation we should so stand before the world as to command the respect and the confidence of mankind. No longer could it be charged upon us that the National Government is the bulwark of slavery; that its legislation is adverse to freedom; that the power of the nation is pledged to perpetuate the system; that it is represented in the National Councils; that the Government shocks